FROM BOSTON TO WARRINGTON

The story of Latchford Albion
ARLFC & their 1953-54 Rugby
League Challenge Cup Campaign

STUART A. McINTOSH

CONTENTS

ACKNOWLEDGMENTS

This brief snapshot of a particular period of Latchford Albion's history was the second in a two-book series and was compiled in 2003.

Several hours were spent in various local library's around the region and the help and patience of the staff there was gratefully received, if not exhausted. All illustrations are reproduced by kind permission of the Warrington Guardian.

The original intention of compiling and producing this slim book was to allow for any proceeds gained to go to the Youth Section of Latchford Albion Unicorns ARLFC. I was proud to have been able to be affiliated with the Unicorns from 1999 until 2007, the majority of which I served as the Youth Section Secretary. Sadly, whilst Latchford Albion ARLFC still exists, the Unicorns have, like the creature they were named after, disappeared from existence.

1. HISTORY REPEATS ITSELF

The Rugby League Challenge Cup competition is one of the world's top sporting events. The tournament was launched at a meeting at Huddersfield in March 1896. Initially it was known as the Northern Union Cup and the first draw was made in September that year. The first final, on 24th April 1897, saw Batley beat St Helens 10–3.

In the early years there was a variety of leagues and it is not easy to distinguish a league club from a non-league club. Gradually the line between professional and amateur clubs became more clearly defined. From 1904 a number of amateur clubs were allowed to compete for qualification to the first-round proper of the Challenge Cup. From 1929 the final, whenever possible, had been staged at the Empire Stadium, Wembley, until its closure.

Unless an amateur club were to meet one of the lowly placed senior clubs in round one their demise as far as the competition is concerned was virtually guaranteed. It was not unheard of for an amateur side to beat a professional one, but it was a rarity. Parton had been the first in 1904 when they beat Millom 8-7 in the preliminary round. From then there had been just six other instances up to the start of the 1953-54 campaign, the last occurrence coming in 1948 when Risehow and Gillhead had beaten Keighley 10-2 in their first round second leg game with Keighley, they had lost the first leg 10-0.

Some amateur clubs had suffered huge scores like the one that crushed the Flimby and Fothergill side in 1925, when the Wigan side piled on 116 points. The legendary Jim Sullivan kicked 22 goals, which is still a record for any competitive match in Britain. The Flimby folk, whose houses fringe the Irish Sea, laughed for many years after about the time their team collected more pounds than points that day.

All this, however, happened twenty years before Latchford Albion had begun playing the sport in the town of Warrington. In our last book, 'When

2

Latchford Albion Made History', the club's formation in 1945 was briefly covered and its first competitive season before going on to explore the 1950-51 Challenge Cup campaign. That was when Latchford Albion made history by becoming the first amateur Rugby League club in Warrington to reach the first-round proper of the Competition.

Rugby League had been played in the town since Warrington had been a founder member of the breakaway Northern Rugby Football Union in 1895. The breakaway from Rugby Union had been on the cards for some time and finally came to a head following a meeting at the George Hotel, Huddersfield on Thursday, 29th August 1895. There were many reasons for the split among which was the desire to give working-class players compensation, or 'broken-time' payments for losing wages in order to play the game. The N. R. F. U. was renamed the Rugby Football League in 1922.

Whilst the newly formed 'professional' game found its feet and developed rules particular to its own code of Rugby, amateur clubs were formed, or existing clubs adapted to take up the new version of the sports. This was the case in the Lancashire town of Warrington. Despite being eligible to compete for entry to the Challenge Cup since 1904, none of the town's amateur clubs had achieved the feat until 1951. That was the year one of the younger clubs, Latchford Albion, managed to win through their seven qualifying games and achieve the honour of meeting top professional side Leigh over two legs.

Having been shown the way by Latchford Albion, Warrington boasted amateur teams in the first round of the Cup for the next two seasons. In 1952 Rylands Recreation Club played Whitehaven and, after losing 16-0 away, Rylands drew 9-9 in their home tie played at Warrington's Wilderspool Stadium. This was only the seventh time an amateur club had drawn with a professional side in the competition. In 1953 Orford Tannery gained the plum draw, when they met Warrington. Both legs were played at Wilderspool and ended 46-2 and 46-8 respectively.

These achievements gave the 1953-54 campaign an added air of anticipation, as local clubs were eager to keep the run going. Additionally, of course, Latchford, Rylands and Orford were desperate to be the first club to extend their history making by becoming the first amateur club in the town to achieve this feat twice.

Latchford began the 1953-54 buoyed by

knowing they were the undisputed champions of the local amateur scene. Latchford Albion, who finished third in the Open Age section of the Warrington Amateur Rugby Football League, became League Champions by defeating Orford Tannery nine points to seven in the last minute of the game at Wilderspool Stadium on Friday, 8th May 1953.

The Albion were the better team, although they lost Ernie Lynskey in the first half through injury.

The Warrington Examiner Newspaper reported: "It was a most interesting game, played in fine sporting manner by two grand teams".

There was plenty of good, open rugby and a finish that kept the spectators keenly interested.

The score was seven points each with only a minute to go as both teams had scored a try and kicked two goals. Latchford's try scorer was Eric Briscoe, Orford's was Adcroft. The goals came from the boots of Ratcliffe for the Tannery and Geoff Kingham for the Albion. The clock was ticking down the last sixty seconds when Johnny Rothwell very calmly dropped a goal to give the Albion a deserved victory.

Both teams had played hard and merited the

congratulations of the League president, Mr. T. Williamson when he presented the cup to the Latchford Albion captain, Geoff Kingham. Medals were also presented to both teams.

This book tells the story of how Latchford Albion built on that success to become the first Warrington amateur club to reach the first round proper of the Rugby League Challenge Cup.

2. THE FIRST STEPS

Every long journey begins with just one step. That first step was to be taken at Victoria Park, Warrington where Latchford Albion played its home games.

When formed, Latchford Albion had played their home games at Chester Road until they moved to Victoria Park off Knutsford Road, Latchford. Victoria Park had been the Old Warps Estate when, in 1897, the Borough Council had bought the fifty-seven acres and created it into a park as part of Queen Victoria's Jubilee celebrations.

Latchford Albion's club headquarters were established at the Black Bear Inn near to Richard Fairclough's School. The team used to change into their playing kit in the barn at the back of the pub before crossing the road to

Victoria Park.

The first qualifying round of the Rugby League Challenge Cup was to be played at 3.00pm on Saturday, 7th October 1953 and their opponents were Penketh Tannery. Only the previous month Penketh had announced that the phenomenal Brian Bevan of Warrington was to be their official coach for the season.

Latchford went into that game having won their opening three fixtures of their League campaign and their first-round game in the Lancashire Cup competition.

Referee Mr. F. Whiteley got the game underway on time and by the interval Penketh had a five point to three lead following a try from Finch and a goal by Whitfield. In the second half Albion took complete control and ran out easy winners scoring 31 points unanswered. Latchford's try scorers were Gordon 'Mickey' Stockton – two, Alf Jackson – two, Len Balshaw, Ron Hennessey, Tony Lagar and Frank Henshaw, while Harry Jenkinson kicked four goals and Geoff Kingham one.

The second qualifying round saw Latchford given another home fixture. This time their opponents were Orrs Zinc White. Naturally, having once reached the first-round proper of the RL Challenge Cup competition, Latchford Albion wanted to repeat the feat. They went a further stage towards it on Saturday, October 24th by defeating Orrs Zinc White by 36 points to 13. The visitors were unfortunate to lose their hooker, Twigg, after just seven minutes' play and he was unable to resume. Despite this severe handicap Orrs Zinc White kept the game interesting, even leading at one stage, but were beaten badly for possession. The Albion were in good form and, despite stout defending from Giles and Martin for the Widnes-based outfit, Latchford were worthy winners.

The draw for the third qualifying round of the Cup included the four remaining members of the Warrington District Area. Widnes' sole surviving amateurs, St Marie's were to play Holmesfield Recreation, while Cadishead and Irlam were to entertain Latchford at their Hollins Green ground. Elsewhere, the St Helens', Wigan and Leigh Districts pitted the winners of Potteries and Grants Hall Colliery (Wigan) against Pilkington Recs (St Helens) and gave Wigan Road Working Man's Club of Leigh a bye.

Latchford Albion were struggling to fit League games into their busy schedule and despite still being unbeaten they found themselves slipping down the table having still only completed their first three fixtures since 12th September.

Instead Latchford were also competing in the Lancashire Cup and managed to qualify for the third round after beating Rylands Recs 27–10.

After two excellent and keenly contested games on Saturday 7th November 1953 St Marie's and Latchford Albion were the teams to go forward to the fourth qualifying round of the Rugby League Challenge Cup competition. One of Latchford's three League victories had been away at Cadishead and Irlam. In that match a number of players had to receive warnings and the referee, Mr. J. Parr, sent off one from each side.

The cup game at Hollins Green was very tough but this time was sportingly played, giving referee Mr. R. Syers a relatively trouble-free afternoon. Cadishead and Irlam led by 8 points to 3 at the interval but Latchford had the advantage in the second half and just managed to get the verdict by 13 points to 10.

Coincidentally, Latchford's next game was the Warrington area semi-final of the Lancashire Junior Cup and the draw meant Latchford had to return to Hollins Green to meet Cadishead and Irlam. The game ended in a draw, but Latchford won the replay 26-7 a fortnight later.

Before that replay Latchford Albion made

further progress towards their Challenge Cup goal on 21st November when they defeated St Marie's at Widnes in the fourth qualifying round. They were now among the last four clubs representing the Lancashire area.

Latchford were full value for their win over St Marie's. In a typical cup-tie battle St Marie's, though striving hard, found the heavier Albion pack too much for them. In the scrums the men from Widnes had the better hooker in Ruane but they were unable to counter the wheeling tactics of their opponents.

The Albion started well and were four points in front after fifteen minutes play from two penalty goals by Alan 'Vince' Whelan, both having been rightly awarded for faulty service of the scrums. For the next ten minutes it was all St Marie's who took the lead with a fine try scored by Potter and converted by Karalius, the latter having also converted a penalty award to give the home team the lead of 7 points to 4 at half time.

Latchford Albion did most of the attacking in the second half, but it was getting late before Tony Lagar scored a smart try to equalise, although the home supporters felt there was a suspicion of offside in its making. From then on it was a dour struggle with St Marie's having a slight territorial advantage. However, with seven minutes to go, Latchford managed to break away and winger Mickey Stockton went over for a good try at the corner. St Marie's tried hard in the last minutes to save the game, but Albion managed to survive strong pressure and ran out winners ten points to seven.

The reward for victory was a home tie to Saddleworth who were from the Oldham area. The venue was switched from the open council-owned Victoria Park to Gorsey Lane, the enclosed home of neighbours, Rylands Recs and the game was played on 5th December.

Although they were the better team, Latchford Albion had a difficult task in beating Saddleworth by seven points to six in the fifth qualifying round of the Rugby League Challenge Cup at Gorsey Lane. It was in the last minute when the visitors missed a penalty kick in front of the posts.

Saddleworth were three points up in seven minutes when Bamford forced his way over for a try. Dyson failed at goal. Geoff Kingham failed with two penalty goals and, although Albion were showing the better combination, they could not penetrate the defence.

Lindley for Saddleworth scored a further

unconverted try in one of their rare visits to the Albion line. From this point Latchford took command and Harry Jenkinson reduced the arrears with a penalty goal. This was quickly followed by a try behind the posts by Danny Jones. Jenkinson then gave Latchford the lead with the conversion making the score 7 points to 6 at the interval.

In the second half, Latchford Albion continued to keep Saddleworth in their own half but after twenty minutes, the referee dismissed Bill 'Ginger' Darbyshire of Latchford. With only one point separating the teams this was a severe handicap and the visitors took advantage to force play to the Latchford line.

A great effort by Ronny Hennessey and Alf Jackson deserved a score, the winger being forced into touch from the corner flag. With a minute to go the visitors were awarded a penalty kick in front of the posts, taken by Dyson. It was a great relief to the home side to see the ball travel outside the posts. It was an extremely hard game with Latchford Albion deserving to win.

Latchford Albion managed to squeeze in a League game before resuming cup duties. They played Widnes-based team, 'Peter Spence' at Victoria Park and proved much too strong, scoring at will in a 47-6 victory. However, all eyes were diverted away from the league programme and, instead, were looking ahead to Saturday 19th December. That was the date when Latchford Albion were going to meet Pilkington Recreation of St. Helens in the sixth qualifying round of the Rugby League Challenge Cup.

The game was another home tie but, again, would not be played at Victoria Park. Instead, the rules dictated the need for an enclosed ground at this stage of the competition and so the game was played at Sandy Lane, the home of Orford Tannery. It had been intended it could be played at Gorsey Lane as the last match had been.

Latchford Albion and Pilkington Recs both already knew that the winners of this match would then play Brookland Rovers of Cumberland in the final qualifying round to decide who was to go into the first-round proper of the competition.

3. THE JOURNEY GATHERS PACE

While some districts were apparently bemoaning a fading interest in Amateur Rugby League football, the Warrington and District League continued to cultivate a live, up to date organisation and the clubs in the area it covered were more than satisfied.

Proof of this was forthcoming at the annual hot pot supper held at the Pelican Hotel, Warrington on Thursday 10th December 1953 when, in addition to the League officials and representatives of the various clubs, there were present Mr. A. Burge chairman of the Amateur League Committee and Messrs. F. W. Daniels (Chairman of Directors), C. Mountford (Manager) and L. Hockenhall (Secretary) of the Warrington Rugby League Club.

That evening also saw Mr. Burge hand out county caps for those players who had represented Lancashire. Among those presented was Geoff Kingham, the Latchford Albion full back. Geoff was a former soccer player who changed codes when Latchford Albion did. He was a founder member of the Rugby League side whose brother was also a particularly good soccer player. Geoff had taken over at full back after the original number one, Billy Daniels, had been prised away from the Albion by the short-lived Walker team.

As early as October 1947 the Warrington Guardian newspaper had singled out Kingham for individual praise under the heading: "*A former soccer player is making his name in Junior Rugby League*". It went on to say how the Latchford Albion full back had played a major part in Albion's win over Farnworth Juniors that season.

Latchford were the league leaders then and routed the Widnes team 68 points to 2 and Kingham had successfully kicked 13 goals out of 14 attempts, making him responsible for 26 of the points scored. At that juncture of the 1947-48 season Latchford had only conceded seven points and had won all five of their league games.

Six years later and Warrington Junior Rugby League club Latchford Albion were experiencing another unbeaten start to the season and, more importantly, had just two more hurdles to surmount before they were in the first round proper of the Rugby League Challenge Cup for the second time in four seasons.

They had a terrific struggle against Pilkington Recs at Sandy Lane, Warrington and it was only dogged determination when faced by an uphill struggle that pulled them through.

Not for the first time during the Cup run Latchford found themselves down at half time. They were losing 7-4 at the interval and were still in arrears with just 15 minutes to go, but finally won 15-12.

Pilkington's played with such confidence and purpose in the opening half hour that Albion rarely got within striking distance of their opponents' line. After eight minutes Rounds opened Pilkington's account when he kicked a penalty goal. This was neutralised by a goal from Kingham after strong forward play had put Latchford into an attacking position and Topping had been penalised for unfair feeding of the scrum. Rounds put his side ahead with a penalty goal before Unsworth made a brilliant break through the centre to send Walsh in with a good try.

Only the most stubborn defence kept Pilkington's out, their forwards being on top in the scrums and loose play and the backs handling smartly. Latchford came back with strong forward bursts and Pilkington's defence was severely tested. The visitors were penalised for deliberately pushing the ball over the touchline and another penalty goal by Kingham just before the interval restored the Albion hopes. With the half time score being 4-7 in favour of Pilkington's a transformation came over the game afterwards.

It was the Albion pack that took command and gradually wore down the opposition. The backs began to show better combination and within a couple of minutes of the restart Jim Marsh went through like a knife for a glorious try at the corner, unconverted by Kingham.

But there was plenty of fight in Pilkington as was proved when Walsh put the finishing touches to a tremendous break after Rigby had intercepted a Latchford pass, had raced clear and supplied a perfect pass for the scorer. Rounds added the goal points.

Offside play under the posts allowed Kingham an easy opportunity to reduce arrears with a penalty goal. Pilkington's were still putting up a good show but their playing of the ball when tackled was feeble, Latchford time after time being allowed to get possession.

Pilkington's were leading by 12 points to 9 with just fifteen minutes left for play setting the stage for a pulsating tussle and so it proved to be. Latchford again found a footing in the visitors' 25 and a feeble attempt at a tackle by Hutton allowed Derek Brocklehurst to force his way over for Kingham to kick the goal.

The home set of forwards was now clearly on top and Pilkington's were kept on defence and it was Kingham who made the issue safe with a penalty goal two minutes from time.

Teamwork put the Albion into the last round but a special pat on the back should be given for a lively set of forwards in which every man did his share. Billy Foden was a great halfback while Geoff Kingham was as steady as a rock at fullback and his goal kicking was invaluable. The St Helens' Reporter newspaper acknowledged that on the day's play Latchford certainly deserved the victory and put this down to "grand goal kicking by Kingham, the Latchford fullback".

Pilkington's just failed to stand the pace, but

they did have two of the best players on the field in Walsh, a clever left-winger and loose forward Unsworth whose brilliance attracted the attention of professional scouts.

Now there was just one more hurdle as Latchford Albion visited Cumberland to meet Brookland Rovers in the seventh, and last, qualifying round and all Warrington wished them well.

4. NEW YEAR RESOLUTIONS

At 5.00 o'clock in the evening on Friday 1st January 1954 fifteen men, including engineers, a tannery worker, an insurance agent, a transport worker and an upholsterer met at the Black Bear Inn to begin a journey which would bring a unique honour to Warrington.

These were the fifteen men of Latchford Albion who were to travel to Cumberland to meet Brookfield Rovers the following day, Saturday 2nd January, in the final qualifying round of the Rugby League Challenge Cup. If they won Warrington would have had a Junior Rugby League Club in the first-round proper of the cup competition for the fourth year in succession.

Six of the players already had experience in the cup against professional sides. Ron Hennessey, Geoff Kingham, Harry Jenkinson, Jim Marsh and Frank Henshaw were in the Latchford team that played Leigh in the 1950-51 season, and Alan Whelan, known to his team-mates as Vince, was in the Rylands' team that played Whitehaven in the following season.

The team had been selected the previous Wednesday night. There was only one change from that which defeated Pilkington Recs in the sixth round. Gordon Stockton, or Mickey as he had been known since his schooldays, had been injured but was now fit again and returned to the left wing instead of Jeff Briscoe.

The team selected was:

Kingham;
Hennessey, Marsh, Balshaw, Stockton;
Foden, Lagar;
Jones
Henshaw, Brocklehurst
Jenkinson, Barlow, Whelan,

Reserves Briscoe and Sixsmith.

The referee was Mr. G. Battersby from Barrow.

A second coach containing non-playing registered players and members left the Black

Bear Inn at 7.45am on the Saturday and joined the players at the Royal Oak Hotel, Keswick before going on to the ground. There were also two coach loads of supporters who made the cold trip through the bleak Lake District and Cumberland fells.

Both teams knew full well the vital issues that were at stake for the winners were to go into the first-round proper of the Rugby League Challenge Cup for only the second time in post-war rugby league. From all accounts, as well as hints drifting from the county of wrestlers and hound trailing, the Rovers were intent on emulating the other Cumberland Junior Clubs who had reached the first round.

Brookland Rovers themselves were no strangers to success in the Challenge Cup. They had already reached the first-round proper on seven occasions and had met Warrington in 1947 when they were beaten 46-3 and 32-3, both games being played at Wilderspool.

The Rovers, with ground advantage, were favourites to win and were boosted by a strong following of supporters encouraging them. The Brookland team were players who had assisted either Workington or Whitehaven such as Thurlow, Maxwell and S. Fearon.

But the Albion also had their stars. Geoff Kingham, the fullback, had played for Lancashire and on three occasions was captain. Ron Hennessey, still only twenty-two years old, was a winger who had played for England Amateurs while Jim Marsh was reserve. Len Balshaw, at centre, was considered at that time to be probably the best of all the Albion three-quarters and he was still three months short of his 23rd birthday.

Mickey Stockton, one of the leading try scorers for the club, was twenty-one years old and, with his forceful running, might prove to be a match winner as he had done against St Marie's in the fourth round. The halfbacks, Billy Foden and Tony Lagar, had blended well together and this clever scheming had brought about the downfall of many clubs.

The captain, twenty-seven-year-old Harry Jenkinson, hooker Freddie Barlow and Vince Whelan formed a formidable front row. Each weighed over 13 stones while Frank Henshaw (12 stone), Derek Brocklehurst (14 stone) and Danny Jones (13st 6lbs) made up the 78½ stones of Latchford brawn and muscle, which was thought to be a match for the granite-like Cumbrian pack.

Brookland won the toss and chose to play with

the wind at their backs and up the slope at Ellenborough. The game kicked off at 2.30pm with a spontaneous attack from the home side, probably designed to knock Latchford off balance. This foundered on the Albion's well-set defence and play was carried back into Brookland territory. Kingham belied his form in recent games by missing a penalty. Shortly afterwards S. Fearon put the Cumberland side ahead with a penalty goal.

This seemed to put heart in to Brookland and inspired them to an incessant attack on the Latchford line, and, at one stage it was only a last-minute tackle that kept the line intact. S. Fearon failed with another penalty attempt, however, and Kingham again missed a chance to level the score with a similar award.

Albion settled down after these early setbacks and Marsh got a grand move going that gave Latchford their first try. He took the ball on his own 25-yard line and sent Hennessey on a swerving run. The wingman evaded a would-be tackler and put in a neat cross-kick to the centre of the Brookland's '25', where Whelan gathered and, in turn, sent out to Stockton, who made no mistake in scoring a try which Kingham failed to improve.

A halt was called to the game at this stage

owing to spectators invading the unfenced touchline. Play was resumed after four minutes and Latchford went into the attack again. All came to naught as the half time whistle blew with the score 2-3 in Latchford's favour.

No doubt Latchford were well lectured at the interval for the second half display made them look a different team. The play of the forwards told more after the interval and Latchford's heavier pack began to call the tune. Barlow, Latchford's hooker, well backed up by his colleagues, gave his side a conveyor belt stream of possession from the scrums, an asset used by the speedy Albion backs.

The turn of the tide came when Tony Lagar instituted a move. Tony was considered a bit too small to make it in the professional game, but he had lightning pace. He went round the blind side from a scrum inside his own '25', he beat several men, showed it to Jimmy Marsh before passing to Ron Hennessey who went over beneath the posts. The referee, however, ruled the final pass to be forward. Len Balshaw was one of several players who questioned Mr. Battersby as he was at least fifty yards behind when the pass was given. All the man from Barrow would say was that to him it seemed forward.

The massive crowd, swelled by there being no games for Workington and Whitehaven that day, seemed to turn at that point in favour of the visitors. Rather than being disheartened the incident proved to be an inspiration and Latchford went straight back into attack with a series of smart passing movements, one of which saw Stockton score his second try. Kingham added the goal points.

More pressure by the Latchford forwards resulted in the same winger completing his hat-trick when he took an inside pass to score behind the posts. Kingham landed the goal. At this point it was all Latchford with nothing to stop them.

Once again, the fitter Latchford side split the tired Brookland defence when Balshaw gave a clever inside pass to Foden who went straight through the gap to score a try that Kingham improved.

The best summary of the game is that it was a triumph of the Latchford club's spirit and physical fitness over a Brookland side that had kept their line intact in the earlier rounds of the competition.

Latchford's Secretary had also ensured they benefited greatly from the gate receipts of an estimated 5,000 spectators once the expenses had been submitted. Tom Clare had taken over as Secretary from his brother Norman, who had become Club Chairman. Tom was an explosive ex-marine with a veracious appetite. On the journey home the coach stopped at the Carnforth Arms, a public house where most teams stopped on their journeys south from the Lake District. Tom asked the landlord if he could cater for fifty-six meals. The landlord offered to cook fifty-six portions of eggs and chips to which Tom is reputed to have replied "Good, there's fifty-five of us and make mine a double portion"!

Latchford's ambition now was to meet the Yorkshire Amateurs in the first-round proper in the hope they could progress into the second round. They also had hopes of pulling off a double by capturing the Lancashire Junior League Cup.

It was not just ambitious thoughts that were racing ahead. The Latchford Albion players, intent on reaching home as quickly as possible after their celebration meal at Carnforth, suffered the indignity of having their coach stopped and the driver booked for speeding. Perhaps the Albion club would pay the driver's fine out of their cup receipts!

FROM BOSTON TO WARRINGTON

5. A PLUM CUP DRAW

It was a couple of weeks later that the draw was made for the first-round proper of the Rugby League Challenge Cup. Thirty-two teams were to play the sixteen first round games.

Latchford Albion were drawn against Wigan. The game would be on a two-leg basis with the matches due to be played on consecutive Saturdays, the 6th February and 13th February.

It was expected that Latchford would apply to the Warrington club for permission to play the second leg on the Wilderspool Stadium. Warrington, however, had been drawn to play Bramley at home in their second leg game on that date. Everyone expected that Wigan would try to come to an arrangement with Latchford whereby the two legs would be switched round and the first leg played at Wilderspool if the Warrington club were willing to loan their ground.

Wilderspool Stadium had been the home of Warrington Rugby League club since 1898. Latchford Albion's first reported game was played there in 1945. Four years later the ground recorded its highest attendance for a league match when 34,304 watched Warrington entertain Wigan. The Warrington club had kindly allowed their historic ground to be used by Latchford for their 1951 Challenge Cup match with Leigh.

Wigan, founded in 1879, were a founder member of the Northern Union. Pre-war they had won the Championship four times and the Challenge Cup twice, whilst being runners-up twice. However, it was in the forties the club experienced real success. They had been Championship winners in the seasons 1943-44, 1945-46, 1946-47, 1949-50 and 1951-52. After being losing finalists in the 1944 and 1946 Challenge Cups, they won the cup in 1948 and 1951. That last victory, beating Barrow 10-0 in 1951, was, of course, the campaign in which Latchford had made it to the first-round proper for the first time.

This is a formidable record by anyone's

standards although, with hindsight, we can see that by 1952 that monumental post-war bonanza was over. The famine after the feast began in the 1952-53 season when for the first time since the war all they had in the trophy cabinet was a runners-up award in the Lancashire Cup Final, after losing 8-16 to St Helens. Hindsight is all well and good but let us not fool ourselves, this was a genuinely great side containing some of the best players in the game at that time.

Also, somewhat significantly, on Friday the 13th March the previous year Wigan had parted with £3,000 for an eighteen-year-old Welsh Rugby Union player, William John Boston.

Billy Boston went on to become one of the best players ever to grace the game of Rugby League. His career for Wigan would span the next fourteen years during which time he was to score 478 tries in 488 games and play in six Wembley finals.

Boston was born on 6th August 1934 in Cardiff's Tiger Bay. He was the sixth of eleven children whose mother was Irish, and their father came from Sierra Leone. Billy had played for Neath Rugby Union Club before National Service took him to the Royal Corps of Signals at Catterick.

Billy was still completing his National Service when he signed for Wigan and was initially only allowed to play during spells of leave from the Signals. For his Rugby League debut in October 1953, 8,500 turned up at Central Park to see him in an 'A' match game against Barrow. They witnessed him score his two tries for the Wigan club.

Billy's full league debut for Wigan was on 21st November 1953 against the same opponents, Barrow. He marked the occasion with a try in the 27-15 victory at Central Park. He scored two more in his second game against Liverpool City, three against Swinton and four in his fourth match against Batley. His opponents for his fifth game in a Wigan shirt were to be...Latchford Albion!

However, in the week before the first leg game the Wigan Observer reported that Billy Boston, their Welsh three quarter, would not be available for the game against Latchford, which had now been switched as expected to Wilderspool for the 6th February. Boston had been chosen to play for the Army Rugby Union team against Cambridge University on that day. Everyone hoped that he would play in the 2nd leg at Wigan on 13th February.

There were other enforced team changes for the

'Cherry and Whites'. Johnny Alty, their scrumhalf had to retire from the match with Warrington on 2nd January with what was at first thought to be a badly bruised shoulder. After closer inspection it was discovered he had dislocated it and he was to be kept in plaster until 18th February.

Wigan also intended for Ronnie Hurst to resume on the left wing in place of Norman Cherrington. Their side would be picked from Cunliffe, Nordgren, Broome, Ashcroft, Hurst, Cherrington, Fleming, T. Parr, Gee, Mather, Williams, Silcock, McTigue and Street. Later in the week Nat Silcock developed a cold and dropped out of contention.

In Warrington all the talk was of Derek Brocklehurst, the Latchford forward, who was rumoured to be about to be snapped up by Leigh. It was certain that had started tongues wagging in the town, but Warrington manager Cec Mountford gave assurances that Albion players would not be poached. New Zealander Mountford had been Wigan's stand-off and captained the club to victory in the Championship in 1950 and in the Challenge Cup in 1951 before taking on the coaching role at Warrington.

The Albion were given full run of the Wilderspool

Stadium for their training sessions. Mountford even absented himself from a Testimonial Sportsman's Night for his Warrington players, Brian Bevan and Bob Ryan, so that he could be with the Latchford players offering them advice for their task as well as to their future in the game.

To most fans the ultimate result of the game was a foregone conclusion in favour of the strong Wigan team, but if the keenness and 100% enthusiasm displayed by Latchford in training was any criterion, Wigan were in for a stiff fight.

The Albion would be without winger Mickey Stockton who was suffering from a torn ligament. This was indeed a blow for the Junior team as Stockton was one of their brightest stars. It was he who scored three tries in Latchford's match at Brookland Rovers in Cumberland.

Jim Marsh also absented himself form the games telling his team-mates that he had already had his moment of glory when he played against Leigh and now it was someone else's turn. Jimmy certainly had enjoyed his time against Leigh playing with true grit, it was he who had jumped on Jimmy Ledgard, injuring the England fullback's leg and putting him out of action for a short time.

Latchford held their final practice on the Wednesday night before the game under the lights at Wilderspool. The pitch was reported to be reasonably fit and had been treated with salt. Hedging his bets, the secretary, Mr. L. Hockenhull said that the match would probably be played.

As the Rugby Union match with Cambridge University and the Royal Signals had been cancelled, Billy Boston would now definitely play in the game.

Latchford decided to employ second row forward, Jimmy Griffiths at right wing to try to counter the new wonder boy from South Wales, while inside Griffiths, Jeff Briscoe was drafted in at centre. Jeff was the younger brother of Eric who also played for the Albion.

6. GETTING TO KNOW YOU

Finally, the strenuous training was over, and the Warrington Junior Rugby League Club were all set for the big kick off at Wilderspool where Latchford Albion were to meet Wigan in the first round, first leg of the Rugby League Challenge Cup. Latchford were not juniors in the matter of years, as their average age was 24, yet is was evident they had been well schooled, and their fitness could not be questioned.

"We are fit and will do our utmost to give the Wigan side a good game" was the comment of the Latchford captain and prop forward Harry Jenkinson and it was with this thought uppermost in their minds that the Junior thirteen took the field.

Those thirteen were:

Geoff Kingham
Jimmy Griffiths, Jeff Briscoe, Len Balshaw,
Ron Hennessey
Billy Foden, Tony Lagar
Danny Jones
Frank Henshaw, Derek Brocklehurst
Harry Jenkinson, Freddie Barlow, Alan Whelan

The Wigan side that took the field was:

Jack Cunliffe
Brian Nordgren, Jack Broome, Ernie Ashcroft,
Billy Boston
Jack Fleming, Tommy Parr
Harry Street
Norman Cherrington, Brian McTigue
Ken Gee, Ronnie Mather, Roy Williams

So, who were these men from Wigan?

Full back, 'Gentleman' Jack Cunliffe was Wigan-born and a product of Newton British Legion. He had two trials with Warrington before signing for Wigan on 11th December 1939 at the age of 17. He was noted for his courage, sportsmanship and all-out effort whenever he played. He was fearless in the tackle and adept at clearing his line with a neat sidestep.

Brian Carl Nordgren or 'Noggy' was a 25-year old law student from New Zealand when he signed for Wigan on 12th December 1945. At the time he signed he held the scoring record in New Zealand Rugby League with 267 points for Ponsonby in the 1944-45 season. He also had success in his home country as a sprinter. This intelligent, articulate and sophisticated man scored two tries in the 1946 Wembley Final defeat but missed six goal kicks, any one of which would have given Wigan victory. He did not kick again for seven years.

Jack Broome was a strong running centre from the West Bank Junior Club in Widnes. He signed in 1948 and proved to be solid and dependable rather than spectacular.

It is said that Ernest Ashcroft was spotted as a 17-year old maintenance fitter playing 'tuck and pass' with a rag ball near the pithead at Maypole Colliery, Abram. He signed on Wigan's books on 20th January 1943, but his raw talent needed honing and he was sent to the White Swan Rangers club in Scholes. After that initial grounding Ernie never looked back and played in the 1943-44 and 1944-45 Yorkshire Cup campaigns and in the two-legged Wartime Challenge Cup final against Bradford Northern in 1944. He became captain of Wigan and England.

Just prior to the game with Latchford, Ashcroft, along with Cunliffe and Nat Silcock, had all been selected for the Great Britain Tour trial.

Jack Fleming had first signed for Wigan on 6th November 1940 from Newton British Legion. He returned in the 1945-46 season from Widnes playing 29 matches and scoring 14 tries. Struggling for a standoff Wigan brought back former player Jack again in 1952. In this final stint he made 47 appearances before finally parting with the Central Park outfit later in 1954 after 47 more games.

Jack's half back partner for this game was to be scrum half Tommy Parr who had come to Wigan from Whelley Boys' Club.

Ken Gee had been the foundation of Wigan's pack almost since the day he joined from Highfield Juniors on 27th October 1933. Respected throughout the world he was in the Great Britain tour parties of 1946 and 1950 and he was considered to be one of the best props of his time. Ken played in ten Lancashire Cup Finals – seven on the winning side – and he also got winners' medals in the Wembley Finals of 1948 and 1951.

Ken's prop partner was Welshman Roy Williams who had come to Wigan from Llanelli Rugby

Union club in 1952.

Despite signing for £50 as a 17-year old from Worsley Boys Club in the 1945-46 season, Ronnie Mather had to wait five years before making his debut. His perseverance was a testimony to the character of a young man who had also been an apprentice centre half for Oldham Athletic Football Club. After a short spell at centre, Ronnie eventually took over the number 9 jersey from the great Joe Egan, a man Latchford Albion knew all too well from their previous encounter with Joe's Leigh side in 1951.

Selected at second row was Norman Cherrington who had signed the previous year from All Saints. Despite his large build he was a fast runner and had been a sprinter in his schooldays. Indeed, most recognised him as the fastest forward in the game.

The other second row forward was Brian McTigue who would undoubtedly have been a professional boxer and had even been invited to the United States to further that career. Boxing's loss was to be Rugby League's gain. The Wigan board saw his potential after only five games as hooker for Giant's Hall Colliery in 1950. He made his Wigan debut in April 1951 and soon found himself being utilised as a second row forward or prop.

Although born near Castleford, Harry Street's first rung on the professional ladder was at St Helens before Dewsbury took him back across the Pennines to team up with his elder brother, Arthur. Harry's four caps on the 1950 Lions' tour attracted the attention of Wigan who were prepared to match the then world record transfer fee of £5,000 to take him to Central Park at the start of the 1951-52 season as part of a dual signing with Len Constance in a deal was said to be worth £8,000. The loose forward was brought in to replace Cec Mountford who had moved to be Warrington's coach.

7. LET BATTLE COMMENCE

In the morning before the game two Wigan directors, Messrs. Wilkinson and Wild journeyed to Wilderspool and, finding the ground generously covered with sand, decided that the conditions were fit to play.

The decision proved to be a wise one as, with it being the only other cup tie in the county and with few counter attractions, there was an attendance of 9,031 yielding gate receipts of £827-10s. No doubt an added attraction was the appearance of the 12st 3lbs, 19-year-old Billy Boston. Had the game been postponed until the following Wednesday it is doubtful if the receipts would have been more than £100. What is more, the crowd got value for their money, as the game was always entertaining and served to warm the cockles on such a bitterly cold day.

Wigan were soon in the lead after only two minutes, when Broome created a clear-cut opening for Nordgren who scored behind the posts for Cunliffe to add the extra points. Nordgren's type of strong running with his knees lifting high had Latchford on the wrong leg from the start although some thought this effort followed a forward pass and he seemed over the dead ball line before grounding. However, that was not the way the referee, Mr. H. Squires from Ossett, saw it.

Latchford showed definite signs of nerves in the early stages and they often kicked with little judgement. This gave Wigan possession which proved fatal as their quick passing and running were most menacing. The men from Warrington had plenty of vocal support and all short incursions into Wigan territory were loudly cheered. Both Kingham and Gee failed with penalty awards before a dropped pass by Nordgren lost him a certain try.

A further score was not long delayed, as from the ensuing scrum, the ball travelled quickly to the opposite flank, where Billy Boston received his first chance to score easily at the corner with just ten minutes on the clock. Cunliffe failed with the kick.

A moment later Billy Boston thrilled the expectant crowd with a forty-yard dash and a great cheer heralded a fine tackle by Geoff Kingham when all seemed lost.

Boston was soon again in action and, in a bewildering run, he beat four defenders before passing inside to Ashcroft whose inability to take the ball lost another scoring chance. Latchford's first real threat came when Frank Henshaw got clean away, but his kick ahead was effectively dealt with by Cunliffe. Briscoe caused further trouble and it was left to Nordgren to save the situation.

Latchford were hereabouts most persistent until McTigue came to Wigan's rescue with a thrilling burst and a timely pass to Cherrington. The move petered out when Wigan were penalised for offside. Quick Wigan passing often had the Albion defence on the wrong foot but much of their good approach work was nullified by faulty finishing.

With twenty minutes of the first half remaining Broome judiciously fed Nordgren near the halfway line. The wingman, with little room in which to work, shook off three attempted tackles and went on to score behind the posts.

Cunliffe kicked an easy goal.

Latchford were seldom in the picture as an attacking force and Cunliffe cut their defence to pieces in a brilliant down-the-middle run. He lacked support but his effort was justly rewarded when McTigue received from the play-the-ball to force his way over. Cunliffe goaled, but only just, as the ball hit the post before going over.

Despite the steadily mounting score, Latchford were still full of fight and their enthusiasm was rewarded when, following a scrum near the Wigan line, Foden got the ball quickly to his right wing, where Jimmy Griffiths not only beat both Boston and Cunliffe, but let them feel his full weight as he sent them both into touch as he put the ball down near the corner for a great try. Jimmy was usually a second row forward and his switch to right wing to marshal the young Boston was inspirational.

Kingham made a poor attempt to improve, but both the home players and their supporters were highly delighted with this success, for which they had waited nearly half an hour. In fact, some might say they had waited a lot longer after failing to score at all in the two games they had played against Leigh at this stage, three years previously.

It was not long, however, before Latchford were further in arrears, for after Cunliffe had kicked a neat penalty goal, Boston smartly gathered a bouncing ball and, after beating a couple of defenders, passed inside to Ashcroft who cantered over. It was too far out for Cunliffe to improve.

The Albion made a quick raid into the Wigan half where Kingham was again wide with a penalty kick. He made amends shortly afterwards when he stopped Nordgren after clever combined play by Parr and Fleming had created a clear-cut opening for the wingman.

Just on half-time Cunliffe gave his side an interval lead of 25 points to 3 with a penalty goal. Experience, superior fitness, skill and weight had told their inevitable tale and the fight appeared to be disappearing from the Albion. Latchford had held their own in the scrums, but little had been seen of their attacking power, although there was merit in their defensive qualities and fighting spirit.

How the British sportsman and sportswoman loves a trier, particularly if facing an unequal task and against a redoubtable opponent. Thirteen amateurs, or to be more precise twelve and one passenger (Kingham, hero of previous rounds through his terrific goal kicking, limped unhappily onto the left wing) not only discovered the spirit to turn the one way traffic into an interesting match, but found three loopholes to supplement a first-half try.

Latchford started the second period in rousing fashion and soon added to their score when Parr was penalised for improperly feeding the scrum – how times have changed. Harry Jenkinson, who had taken over the kicking duties from the injured Kingham, landed an easy goal.

Latchford were eager for more points and their persistent attack on the Wigan line was giving their fans plenty to shout about. Within six minutes of the resumption there was a quick change of operations however, when Boston gathered a short kick through from the full back and raced away from his own line to score under the posts.

Those who had come to see Billy Boston in action must have realised by this what a power he was going to be in the game. He was tall, powerful and speedy, weighing in at that time at just 12st 3lbs. What was more pleasing to his club was that he was showing quick and keen adaptability to the new code. As a straight runner he impressed, but in this game, he seemed inclined to favour the 'rounding' of an opponent rather than the unorthodox subterfuge. The Wigan press suggested that the left winger found that the slippery under surface of the ground negated his devastating side-step forcing him to rely mainly on straight running with a change of pace or a hand-off. Certainly, Boston without his side-step was not fully effective.

Kingham had nabbed him well before the Welshman claimed sweet revenge with his ninety-yard run for his second try in which he easily outpaced the Latchford three-quarters. As he sped along the touchline it was delightful to see Boston's graceful running action, which made try-scoring look easy.

Those who were seeing him for the first time thought him not quite as fast as the great Brian Bevan of Warrington, although allowances had to be made for the Army duties Billy was still performing. It was acknowledged that as soon as he was able to spend a great deal of time on training and study of Rugby League methods more closely, Boston would put on a yard or two. The more discerning punter would wait for the opportunity to study his talents when faced with sterner opposition before passing judgement.

Cunliffe revealed himself as an efficient goal kicker. He added the extra points and, with an eye on openings, was deserving of a Tour place. After a new ball had been demanded, good work by Williams and Parr gave Boston a further chance, but this time he was overwhelmed near the corner flag. Before the scene changed Parr sent Cherrington over for Cunliffe to again add goal points.

A dazzling Wigan movement in which backs and forwards participated was more than the Albion could cope with and, when Nordgren received near the half way line he brushed past Kingham, who appeared bewildered by the effort, to touch down near the posts. Cunliffe's goal gave Wigan a 35-points lead.

There was no suggestion of any remarkable turn of events for at 40-5 Wigan looked like adding another ten or twenty points without reply. With 25 minutes left for play it looked like being distinctly uncomfortable for the amateurs.

But then the chunky and industrious Brocklehurst made a brilliant burst that had the Wigan defence all at sea. It was just the lead the amateurs had been waiting for. Down the middle he went like a forceful centre showing his real mettle. It looked like being one of the tries of the day, but the otherwise quick-thinking second row forward elected to kick.

A pass might have meant all the difference in the world for the athletic-looking Billy Foden, who appeared to be the real part as a standoff, was positioned for a pass. None came as Brocklehurst booted pass Cunliffe towards the posts.

Foden did not throw up his hands in despair but chased the punt and got his hands to the ball before it cannoned off the post and into the welcome grasp of a Wigan player. Such a grand effort deserved a better fate and it could quite easily have been five more points to Latchford. They did get some reward when, in the next minute, Jenkinson kicked a penalty goal before Wigan could regain the lost ground.

This was indeed the incentive for the Albion players and from this stage until the end it was all Latchford. With the crowd howling louder than it did at some Warrington first team fixtures, play hung around the Wigan line for some time. The way they hammered away at the Wigan line was indeed proof of Latchford's fighting qualities and fitness.

With hooking level and Wigan doing nothing in the way of reproducing the sparkling movements leading to the earlier Nordgren and Boston tries, there was an air of expectation about the Juniors' fortunes. Cunliffe was constantly in action, dealing with the many threatening situations. Success came again and trust the amateurs to show their 'superiors' a thing or two.

Freddie Barlow struck cleverly as a good hooker should and his colleagues healed so smartly that Tony Lagar was able to slip around the scrum and kick over the Wigan line. Cunliffe, under his own posts missed the awkward bounce, and Danny Jones was quick to follow up, touching down near the posts with two Wiganers looking on. The crowd roared, and roared again, as Jenkinson converted.

Latchford rode their luck when Boston, after another thrilling run, passed inside to Fleming, who, had he accepted the chance, would have scored with little difficulty. Cunliffe then went near with a penalty kick. Back went the Albion realizing full well that this was indeed their glory day. Snappy passing on the right and perilously near the sideline saw Jones once again in the right place. Immediately he got the ball he swung it down to the line amid another deafening cheer.

Just to show there was no luck about their methods Jenkinson banged over as neat a goal as you could wish to see from almost on the touchline.

Crowding tactics gave Wigan little or no opportunity to leave their quarters and yet another blow came as Ron Hennessey switched from the left and swung into a passing movement which had Wigan beaten. So much so that Hennessey was almost unchallenged as he fairly romped over in the corner. Jenkinson's kick from far out went inches wide.

When the final whistle sounded, the Wigan players were not slow to congratulate their opponents on a great second half display.

8. AS THE DUST SETTLED

It could be suggested that Wigan eased up after compiling such a commanding lead, but if they did it was anything but obvious. They could, however, be excused for not taking any unnecessary risks on the hard ground when they had the game well in hand.

Wigan never took the same risks as the junior side on the hard bone-shaking ground, but Latchford must still be congratulated on their enterprising rally in the second half in which they took the score 40-5 to 40-20, 15 points without reply. Their points came from enthusiasm rather than skill, although the third try by lanky loose-forward Danny Jones from which captain Harry Jenkinson kicked a great touchline goal was gained by astute passing from a play-the-ball movement close to the Wigan line. It earned a great ovation.

A mere mention of the fact that Warrington Amateur Rugby League teams had reached the Challenge Cup first round proper on the last four occasions should offer enough evidence that Junior Rugby in the town was far superior to that of other districts. If this claim should be disputed, then the outcome of the Latchford Albion – Wigan first leg game at Wilderspool can be quoted to support that contention.

It would take some research to discover whether an amateur side had ever registered so many points against a senior thirteen in the competition up to that game, but the Albion, who were making their second post-war appearance in the tourney, won all-round admiration for their rearguard action, which eventually turned into an all-out assault.

Observers were in no doubt that on the whole Wigan played in top gear without needing acceleration, but perhaps this team was not as snappy and purposeful as the Wigan of old. What Silcock and Alty would have done against Latchford is a matter of conjecture but one Wigan supporters could not help thinking about. The Wigan pack missed the power of Nat Silcock in the second row, who was absent with a cold, and generally they played second fiddle to the Latchford six.

Bumps and knocks were taken in all good spirit and the way the Wiganers took the initiative to compliment the Juniors on their showing revealed true sportsmanship. Ashcroft's efforts to personally congratulate every Albion hero before he left the field was a gesture which was not only appreciated by the crowds but an action unlikely to have been forgotten for a long while.

The absence of stars Gordon 'Mickey' Stockton and Jim Marsh did not upset the Albion as much as was first thought. The thirteen were heroes one and all and while we should be reluctant to individualise after such a brave show, Jack Steel of the Warrington Guardian newspaper thought Derek Brocklehurst was a player with a big future.

The Wigan Observer also acknowledged second row forward Brocklehurst suggesting Latchford had their very own Nat Silcock and reminding their readership that Derek had twice shown amazing speed to scatter the Wigan defence. They suggested that with better support both efforts might have brought a try. They perpetuated the rumour that Leigh had signed him for trial.

However, the paper felt that the forward honours among the Albion team should go to the ubiquitous Harry Jenkinson who worked tirelessly for the full eighty minutes. They added: "In the role of captain and tactician he fared worse, too often calling upon Kingham to attempt goal kicks when the chances were very slender. He would have done well to have emulated Ashcroft whose captaincy of the Wigan team is improving with every game". Ironically, Jenkinson himself took over the goal kicking after Kingham's injury and was successful four times. It was true that Ashcroft looked good for another trip overseas.

Freddie Barlow won a lot of credit for holding his opposite hooker, Mather, to a 16-15 win in the scrums.

Main source of worry to the Latchford defence was the speed and power of Nordgren and Boston on the wings. They scored five tries between them and Nordgren, with a better service from Broome, whose passes were sometimes badly timed, might have had more than three. In fairness to Broome, however, it must be said that Nordgren dropped some passes, which he should have safely collected.

Jack Cunliffe found it difficult to affect his side-step. Accustomed to clearing his line with a swerving run and a side-step, Cunliffe slipped at almost every attempt. Once a player started on a particular path it was hard to change direction. But, with his flair for adaptability, he discarded individual attack and changed to concerted movements with his three-quarters. He was again on grand goal-kicking form, kicking eight goals.

In combating slippery grounds, it was suggested that perhaps Wigan would do well to obtain some of the rubber soled boots, which several Latchford players wore. The real things had the studs molded on to the rubber sole. This gave resilience, which was the secret of the boots. However, it must be said that the somewhat flimsy footwear put paid to Billy Foden's chances of playing in the return leg after Ken Gee had trodden on his foot, breaking his toe.

Although Latchford Albion had virtually no chance of entering the second round of the Challenge Cup supporters who planned to go to Central Park for the second leg on Saturday, 13th February 1954 were ensured of seeing a game display of enthusiasm and tireless spirit. That much was certain if Latchford repeated the performance that they gave in the first leg at Wilderspool.

Central Park had been grazing land until Wigan Rugby League Club acquired it on 6th September 1902. It became one of the most famous venues for sport in Britain. The record attendance at the ground was 47,747 for a league game against St Helens in 1949, which was also the record attendance for any league game in Britain. The ground had hosted the Challenge Cup Finals in 1927, 1928 and 1932. In the 1952-53 season it was decided to build a modern stand on the Popular Side of the ground and to cover the Spion Kop. The old 'Dutch Barn' was then removed.

In the week leading up to the second leg game it was announced that Wigan had dropped Norman Cherrington from their team. They still hoped to have Boston available and, although Cunliffe was included in the squad, he was likely to be rested. That meant Don Platt would play full-back. Don had been signed from Bickershaw Colliery in 1952.

Drafted into the pack was Wigan-born Bill Collier, the brother of another Wigan player, Frank. Bill was another product of the Worsley Boys' Club and had been at the Central Park club since 1950.

Ken Gee was reported to be suffering from a feverish cold, making him doubtful for the cup-tie. However, giant second row forward, Nat Silcock had recovered from his cold and was included in the squad. Nat was named after his father, a Great Britain International who had played for Widnes. Nat junior had joined Wigan from the Widnes junior club, West Bank, in 1947. He had already won winners' medals in the Championship (1950 and 1952), the Challenge Cup (1951) and the Lancashire Cup (1948, 1950 and 1951).

Injuries necessitated several changes in the Latchford ranks. Alf Jackson was to replace Ron Hennessey on the left flank, while the wingman moved into the centre to occupy Len Balshaw's place. Billy Foden dropped out from stand-off half with a foot injury so Balshaw was to take his place. Freddie Barlow had received an ankle injury and Bill 'Ginger' Darbyshire deputised as hooker.

The referee for this game was Mr. R. Gelder from Wakefield, while the sides lined up for the second-leg game as follows: -

WIGAN
↓

Don Platt

Brian Nordgren, Jack Broome, Ernie Ashcroft,
Ronnie Hurst

Jack Fleming, Tommy Parr

Harry Street

Nat Silcock, Brian McTigue

Ken Gee, Bill Collier, Roy Williams

Alan Whelan, Bill Darbyshire, Harry Jenkinson,

Derek Brocklehurst, Frank Henshaw

Danny Jones

Tony Lagar, Len Balshaw

Jimmy Griffiths, Ron Hennessey, Eric Briscoe,
Alf Jackson

Geoff Kingham

↑
LATCHFORD ALBION

9. THE JOURNEY ENDS

Conditions for Latchford Albion's second leg cup-tie with Wigan were vastly different from the previous week, Central Park being ankle deep in mud. In consequence play was often scrappy and with the game already 'in the bag' from Wigan's point of view there was a lack of the usual cup-tie enthusiasm.

Billy Boston was engaged in an important Army game the following Tuesday and so he was not allowed to play in this game. Ronnie Hurst took his place. Hurst had been on Wigan's books since 1949, having arrived from Pembroke Rovers. The feats of Boston had perhaps helped to push Hurst into the background but in truth Wigan had in Hurst an excellent servant whom many another club would have been glad to have on their register.

As expected, Platt and W. Collier had come in for Cunliffe and Mather who were rested. Silcock was included in the forwards to the exclusion of Cherrington.

Ascroft was again in brilliant form with Fleming giving a much-improved display. Gee's goal kicking being another feature. It must be said that Latchford were outclassed but stuck manfully to their task and again earned praise for their never-say-die spirit.

Wigan at once took up the running when Street picked up a loose ball to feed Parr who soon found the heavy going a handicap and was unable to make ground. Ashcroft was more successful when he weaved his way through to be stopped near Latchford's line. Here Albion were penalised and Platt had no difficulty adding two further points to Wigan's aggregate lead with only three minutes gone.

Kingham made a good attempt at the other end when Parr was penalised at the scrum. This was the start of an onslaught on the home line, which ended when Silcock's burst took play to midfield. The Latchford forwards, with Brocklehurst often in the picture, were showing plenty of spirit but they found the tackling of the Wiganers more tenacious than the previous week. It was not easy to find a gap in their defence.

Still, they were winning plenty of the ball from the scrums but the handling and passing of their back division was erratic. It was this fault that led to Wigan going further ahead on six minutes. Parr's interception gave him an unopposed run to the line. Gee failed with the kick.

Latchford fought back with commendable spirit and a clever combined movement by Balshaw and Lagar threatened danger and, before Wigan could ease the pressure, they were penalised. Kingham again got close with his kick. Street and Williams were instrumental in getting Nordgren away, but Griffiths stopped his progress very effectively.

Platt was called upon to save twice in quick succession behind his line, but Wigan quickly changed defence into attack when Ashcroft burst through smartly to feed Hurst near midfield. The wingman in a long run left the opposition behind to cross for a try, which Gee improved with a great kick.

Latchford, although still winning plenty of the

ball, often nullified this advantage through faulty handling and badly directed passes. Their forwards, however, often worried the Wigan defence and McTigue was twice hard pressed to save during a lively onslaught on his line.

Fleming and Ashcroft were a lively pair and many of the home attacks were initiated by them, the latter proving a fine partner for Hurst, who again thrilled the crowd with a long touchline run in which he non-plussed the opposition to score in grand fashion. Gee goaled again.

Wigan were well up on top now and a quick burst by Parr saw Fleming take an awkward pass in smart fashion to race clean away to ground the ball under the post. The referee, Mr. Gelder however, decided that the transfer was forward, but it must have been a near thing.

Nordgren, in fact, had seen little of the ball, but when he did eventually get half a chance in his own half, he spread-eagled the defence to score a characteristic try. Gee added the extra points with another fine kick.

Thirty-three minutes had elapsed and, somewhat understandably, Latchford had now lost much of their early vigour. Although one had to admire their fighting spirit with odds so heavily against them and when the interval was signalled they were a further twenty points in arrears.

Ashcroft, who had created many scoring opportunities in the opening half, was soon in action when the game resumed but Platt, whose play in attack had not been up to its usual standard, ruined an early chance by serving out a wretched pass.

Although play was confined to the Latchford half for a long period their line was rarely in danger and it was the Albion who came nearest to scoring. The movement started from a scrum on the halfway line and surprisingly enough when Wigan hooked the ball.

Parr fumbled and Jones, Latchford's loose-forward, whipped 'round the scrum and, with a hefty boot, sent the ball scudding towards the Wigan fullback. Platt seemed to have all the time in the world to pick up, but he hesitated – a fatal mistake against enthusiastic juniors – and along came Tony Lagar to kick the ball off the point of his nose.

The ball rolled slowly across the Wigan line with Lagar and Broome in hot pursuit. Betting on the winner was even but a nudge by Broome's left shoulder was enough to upset Lagar and with a powerful shot Broome hoofed the ball into the crowd.

Shortly after this Latchford registered their only score when Wigan transgressed the offside rule under their own posts and Kingham kicked the goal with 7 minutes of the second half gone. Kingham made an improvement on his display at Wilderspool and the two penalty shots from near the touchline were only just wide of the mark. His lack of weight was apparent, however, as Nordgren brushed passed him on several occasions.

Latchford found a new lease of life for a while but against effective Wigan tackling there were no signs of another Albion revival, but their fighting spirit was still evident. Ashcroft and Fleming continued to tear holes in their defensive armour and with Nordgren always a menace when in possession Latchford were sorely tried. As the second half progressed Latchford naturally tired and the fine sweeping movements by the Wigan backs repeatedly cracked the Albion defence.

On the hour Wigan began a series of rapid scoring. Nordgren fed Broome who scored, and

Gee goaled. Nordgren scored himself two minutes later when Fleming picked up a dropped pass and let in Noggy who rounded Kingham to touch down. Ashcroft cantered over for another. Platt then ran in under the posts and converted himself.

Fleming limped off and was replaced at stand off by Ashcroft. Street then swept through and after several passes the ball came to Nordgren who scored his hat trick. Gee kicked his fifth goal to finish off the scoring.

Despite their severe hammering Latchford found strength to stage a last-minute rally and as the final whistle sounded, they were fighting hard for a try. Latchford were decisively beaten but were not disgraced.

10. A FINAL POST MORTUM

Despite the fine form shown by Latchford Albion in the first leg of their first round Rugby League Challenge Cup tie with Wigan at Wilderspool and their breathtaking second-half rally many people expressed the opinion that the result at Central Park would be a cricket score. Those fears were almost true.

The 100% enthusiasm and fighting spirit by the Albion were still there, but their skill in passing and tigerish ferocity displayed at Wilderspool was left behind with the majority of their supporters.

The Central Park pitch was very heavy, but instead of bringing Wigan down to Latchford's speed it was Latchford who were bogged down. The heavy state of the ground soon got churned up into a morass and did bog down the Wigan attack in the second half. A white ball was used but this only seemed to accentuate Albion's handling errors and it was quite galling to see the forwards gaining a good share of the ball, but many promising movements breaking down through bad passes or knock-ons.

It was perfectly obvious from the onset that Wigan were not going to Latchford to shake them out of their stride for a second week and the softening process started from the first whistle, when the Latchford forwards were dumped unceremoniously in the mud as soon as they received the ball. Latchford, too, appeared to thoroughly enjoy slapping Wigan players into the thick clinging mud; halfback Tommy Parr took quite a drubbing.

Latchford's enthusiasm led in part to their own undoing. They were so eager to get at the Wigan man with the ball swooping down on him like a lot of happy, yapping terriers that defenders were repeatedly pulled out of position.

Those hardy characters Derek Brocklehurst and Frank Henshaw, stars of the Wilderspool battle, were well policed and despite constant probing were unable to find any loopholes for their dashing solos. Wherever the battle raged fiercest these two could be found and Henshaw repeatedly took the eye with some judicious kicking.

Star of the Latchford back division, which was repeatedly hoodwinked by that wily campaigner Ashcroft, was scrumhalf Tony Lagar who kicked and ran well throughout the whole match.

Geoff Kingham also took playing honours in the Latchford ranks. He put up a game show at fullback and kicking with his left foot was three times only inches off the mark with goal kicks from wide angles before he finally kicked the second half goal which represented Latchford's points tally in the game.

The attendance of 8,139 was considered satisfactory, yielding receipts of £597-16s-3d. However, it was never about the money. That was a nice bonus for the amateurs from Latchford. Instead it was more satisfying that Latchford had managed the fantastic achievement of beating seven opponents to earn the right to compete in their chosen sport against one of the best clubs in the game. Not only that, but to make history by becoming the first amateur club from Warrington to achieve this feat twice was outstanding.

There was also personal recognition for a couple

of Latchford's players:

Derek Brocklehurst went on to play for Warrington. Harry Bath of Warrington took a fancy to him and signed him for Warrington, although he only played a couple of games. He secured a job working for Cubitts building firm and moved to Ireland where he was earning three times as much as he did by playing Rugby.

William A. 'Billy' Foden lived in Plinston Avenue, Latchford and played stand off for Eagle Sports in Warrington as well as Latchford Albion. The manager of professional outfit, Blackpool was Chris Brocklehurst who was a former Wires' man. He signed Billy for Blackpool.

The history-making of Latchford Albion did not finish there, but maybe that is best left for another book...

FROM BOSTON TO WARRINGTON

BOOKS IN THIS SERIES

The early history of
Latchford Albion ARLFC

Latchford Albion are an amateur Rugby League team from Warrington in Cheshire who became the first local amateur club to progress to the first round proper of the Rugby League Challenge Cup in the 1950-51 season leading to their meeting with the then mighty Leigh.

Two years later Latchford Albion made history again when they achieved the feat for a second time. Their opponents this time for the two-legged cup-tie were the legendary Wigan.

When Latchford Albion Made History...is the story of a fledgling Rugby League team from Warrington who became the first local amateur club to progress to the first-round proper of the Rugby League Challenge Cup in the 1950-51 season.

ABOUT THE AUTHOR

Stuart A. McIntosh was born in Saudi Arabia to parents stationed there with the Royal Air Force. They returned to the UK, but Stuart's father died shortly before Stuart's sixth birthday, which ultimately led to him being educated at a boarding school in the Midlands. Stuart became a Police Officer in the North West and, after thirty years' service, worked for the local council and the Home Office in investigator roles.

It is this upbringing that colours his poems that have been published in several books throughout his adulthood.

Stuart was also a keen sportsman in his younger day and his associations with local amateur sports clubs led him to compile two histories of a local amateur Rugby League Club and create a history of a local amateur Cricket Club.

He has also edited and contributed to other publications

Printed in Great Britain
by Amazon

57845349R00050